Notice:

_____

Table of Contents

WHY YOU NEED THIS BOOK

My seven and ten year old sons and I put together *Nerf War* in order to help other Nerf fans to find some new and exciting ways to enjoy these fantastic products and come together as families in the process.

The temptation for many young Nerf gunners will be to jump right into the chapters where we field test the blasters and accessories. That is going to be the best part of the book for most readers!

We will talk about all of your favorite blasters and discover which ones shoot the farthest, fastest and straightest. Want to be a Nerf sniper?? We will show you which blasters are the best for your sniper perch, allowing you to take out your friends from over 100' away with deadly accuracy.

Perhaps you need a back-up weapon, one that you can conceal under your Nerf tactical vest, in case you get taken prisoner (been there, done that!). We will cover many different models of Nerf and Buzz Bee blasters, so that you can decide which blasters to add to your arsenal.

For many of these blasters, we will provide actual field tests. We will fire the blasters and measure how far they *really* shoot. We will test accuracy. And, probably most importantly, we will provide actual opinions from kids that own the blasters. Which do they like best? Which blasters do they use for specific battles? What are the pros and cons of some of the most popular models?

But, in addition to the product specs and reviews, we are also going to talk about a lot of other important things that go along with Nerf wars that children and parents can read together.

We will talk about Nerf war safety, which is very important to parents and, let's face it, your wars will be more fun if nobody gets hurt and there are no arguments about the rules. We will also offer some excellent ideas on new ways to set up foam dart blaster battlefields and methods for getting other family members involved in the fun.

You will also read some accounts from actual Nerf wars. Some stories are funny, some are great shots or smart battle plans. All of the stories are entertaining. You will see actual photos of Nerf blasters in action.

We even talk about Nerf blaster mods – should you modify or customize your favorite blaster…? We will talk about why you might want to mod your blaster and also offer reasons why it may be best not to alter them at all.

Finally, we will talk about some ways that you can pick up blasters, replacement parts and accessories for great prices. Why pay $40 for a brand new blaster, when you get one that has only been used a couple of times for under $3?

Before we start, I just want to take a moment to ask my fellow Nerf fans to go to the review page after you have read this book and leave a review. Excellent reviews are very helpful for potential readers who are considering buying this book and the proceeds from the sales of this book go straight into my sons' college funds.

Well… let's get on with the blasting!

NERF HISTORY AND NERF BASICS

Impress your friends. What does the acronym N.E.R.F. actually stand for?

The answer... Non Expanding Recreational Foam.

The idea for Nerf toy products was originally inspired by the foam that was being used on accessories for recreational vehicles like jeeps. Nerf bars are used on the bottoms of vehicles to prevent damage and so that people can get into jacked up vehicles easier.

In 1970, Parker Brothers started production of the original Nerf ball. The ball was a simple hand-sized round ball. The marketing slogan (according to Nerf Wikia.com) was "Throw it indoors... You can't hurt babies or old people."

Nerf balls were an immediate hit, selling over 4 million balls in the first year. Soon afterwards, Parker Brothers released Super Nerf Ball, a larger version of the original Nerf ball and then the favorite Nerf product of all time, the Nerf football was offered for sale in 1972.

The first Nerf blaster was released in 1989. Known as Blast-a-Ball, the blaster shot a ball by pumping the handle forward. Shortly after that, the Nerf Bow 'n' Arrow was released in 1990 to great fanfare. Nerf initially tried several models of blasters that fired large missiles, but poor performance led to the discontinuation of these models in 1994.

Also in the early 1990s, Nerf was purchased by Hasbro Toy Company and they took over manufacture of the entire product line.

In 1992, Hasbro issued its first modern Nerf dart blaster, the Nerf Sharpshooter. The Sharpshooter was a hand-held blaster that fired medium sized darts with fins on their backs. It was an immediate success and a big seller.

In the 1990s and early 2000s, many dart-shooting models were tested and scrapped and the process led to the formation of many of the exciting high-performance blasters that can be bought today.

Several lines of darts have been added, including the larger Mega darts, whistling darts, and Zombie Strike darts. In 2012, Nerf developed the N-Strike blasters and the Elite dart became the standard dart used in blasters.

In 2011, Nerf added a new line of blasters that shot round foam discs, instead of darts. Disc shooting blasters were first sold in the 1990s, but they failed. They re-emerged successfully in 2011, with Nerf's popular Vortex series of disc shooters.

In 2013, Nerf added the Rebelle, a blaster marketed towards girls. The Rebelle has been met with mixed opinions.

In 2011, Nerf won the Boy Toy of the Year with the Stampede ECS and Outdoor Toy of the Year with the Shot Blast blaster.

Currently, Amazon lists over 1500 items for sale related to Nerf blasters.

Nerf Blaster Basics

There are some things that we need to talk about before we get into the nuts and bolts of Nerf blasters, so that we can understand each other better. We do not have to be engineers to discuss Nerf blasters, but it is much cooler if we all have a working knowledge of how the blasters work and what the parts are called.

First, let's get into how Nerf blasters actually work. We will keep this really simple, so younger kids can understand. Nerf blasters operate because of two working parts – the spring inside the barrel and the release of compressed air.

It works like this:

1. There are two tubes inside most Nerf shooters. Both tubes are hollow. One tube has a cap on the end closest to the stock. Behind the cap is a spring. The larger and thicker the spring is, the faster the blaster will shoot the dart out.

2. There are many varieties of blasters, and they use several different methods in order to cock the blaster and get it ready to shoot. But, in each type of blaster, the blaster is prepared to shoot by cocking the blaster. Inside the blaster, a plunger tube is pulled back and the spring is compressed, storing energy for the shot. When the blaster is cocked, it is

locked into place with an interior cocking mechanism. The blaster is then ready to fire.

3. When the person holding the blaster pulls the trigger, the cocking mechanism is released. The spring pushes the plunger tube forward at a very high rate of speed. The plunger tube creates air pressure inside the barrel of the blaster and that forces the dart out of the muzzle of the blaster.

There are many other ways that blaster actions can be constructed, so that air pressure is built up inside the barrel, but the firing principles are similar.

As we discussed before, the speed and distance that a Nerf blaster can fire is based on how much air pressure can be built up inside the barrel when the trigger is pulled. This can be increased in several different ways:

1. Making the spring tighter or longer increases the "push" behind the plunger.

2. Making the chamber seal tighter, so less air pressure escapes when the trigger is pulled.

3. Artificially increasing the air pressure inside the plunger, using other mechanisms inside the blaster.

After you have fired a couple of different Nerf blasters, you will notice that longer barreled blasters like sniper rifles can often generate more air pressure inside the blasters than short barreled models, such as hand-held pistols. Why is that?

You guessed it! The longer tube inside the barrel allows more air to be compressed and generates more compressed energy before the trigger is pulled. The same thing is true of adult firearms. Rifles can usually shoot faster and farther than pistols.

Now, let's talk about some terminology. *Terminology* means the words and definitions used by a group of people when talking about a particular subject.

First, we will talk about the parts of a Nerf blaster. In your mind, picture a long blaster, like a sniper rifle. Start from the back of the blaster.

The piece of the blaster that goes against your shoulder is the **stock**. The stock allows you to hold the blaster firmly and aim it, while you pull the trigger. The stock can be long, as in the case of a rifle, or short, like the Zombie Strike blasters.

The **action** is the portion of the blaster that you have to move in order to cock it. There are several different types of actions, including bolt action, pump action and lever action mechanisms. The action can be located near the trigger, or it can be a pump or lever closer to the barrel of the blaster.

The **barrel** is the tube that the projectile comes out of. Again, the barrel can be long for rifles, or much shorter for pistols. Some blasters have multiple barrels that can each hold a dart that will be fired when the trigger is pulled.

The **muzzle** is the very end of the blaster. It is the hollow tube that the dart is fired from. The muzzles in modern toy blasters are required to be painted orange, so that they are not mistaken for real adult guns.

Many blasters use **clips** to hold the darts. The clip holds up to 24 darts and is often inserted into a hole in the bottom of the blaster near the trigger. Many Nerf gunners carry extra clips during Nerf wars, so that when the first clip runs dry, they can quickly replace it with a new clip that is full of darts.

It is very important to know which types of **darts** the blaster fires before it is bought. Many blasters have darts that are *interchangeable* with many other blasters. This means that the same darts can be used in different models of blasters. Many of the modern Nerf blasters use the N-Strike Elite dart. However, there is also a line of blasters that use the larger **Mega darts**.

We will talk more about the types of darts later in the book, but it is important to understand that all Nerf blasters do not shoot the same darts. And, other manufacturers like Buzz-Bee and BoomCo have their own darts that often cannot be used in Nerf blasters and vice versa.

Action Types in Foam Blasters

There are several ways that modern foam dart blasters can be cocked, in order to prepare the blaster so that it can shoot.

Many blasters are cocked using a **bolt action**. A bolt action cocks the blaster by pulling back a bolt, which is usually located near the trigger. Some models have an actual "bolt" that looks similar to a real blaster. Others have a sliding bolt with a large handle, like the Mega Centurion. Some Buzz-Bee sniper models, like the Extreme Rangemaster, have a pumping bolt that allows you to cock the action multiple times to build pressure inside the tube.

Another popular type of action is the **pump action**. The action can be located in different areas of the blasters, but often it is either just in front of the trigger, or it may be near the muzzle at the end of the blaster (like with many disc shooters). With the pump action, the blaster is cocked by sliding a mechanism back and forth.

There are also a number of models that are cocked with a **lever action.** The lever is often located below the trigger. The action is operated by lifting the lever away from the blaster and then cocking it back against the blaster to load it. Many older Nerf models use this type of action and there are several types of lever action Buzz-Bee blasters that can be cocked multiple times to increase the air pressure and shoot faster.

Several pistols and older models use a **slide action**, where the blaster is cocked by sliding the entire casing of the blaster back and then forward again in order to cock them. Some pistol models also use a pull ring at the back of the blaster as a cocking device.

NERF BLASTER SAFETY

Ah, the chapter that most parents have been looking for.

But, this chapter is also for gunners, because gearing up with safety equipment can also add to the Nerf war experience! Luckily, lots of the gear is super sweet, so you can look more like real soldiers by wearing the clothing and accessories that keep you and your friends from getting hurt.

Let me start by saying that Nerf products are tested thousands of times before they are released, so that they don't hurt kids or break fragile items. If these blasters are used properly, it is very rare for kids to get hurt by being hit with a Nerf dart. The darts are soft and the blasters that are bought from the stores do not shoot fast enough to do more than sting a bit.

We will talk more about "modding" blasters later, but blasters that are modified CAN in fact shoot fast enough to bruise people and break glass items, so this is another reason you may decide not to alter the blasters.

We are going to talk about several ways to have safe Nerf battles:

1. Safe Handling of Blasters
2. Firing Safety
3. Protective Gear and Battlefield Safety

Safe Handling of Blasters

Improper handling of blasters can result in minor injuries to the user. Pinched fingers and broken fingernails can easily be prevented by reading the user manuals for the blasters before shooting them. If you bought the blaster used, you can still download many manuals for newer blasters for free on the Hasbro website at http://www.hasbro.com/nerf/en_US/discover/instructions-search.cfm?N=252+63+861.

The user should be familiar with how the action of the blaster works in order to avoid pinching fingers in the action of the blaster. Never put hands or fingers inside the parts that cock the blaster. In other words, don't hold onto the blaster where the pump action slides when you are cocking it.

And, most importantly, don't ever look down the muzzle of the blaster – ever! Even if you are positive that the blaster is unloaded, you should not put your eye near the area that shoots the projectile.

Most modern blasters are designed so that there is no reason to look down the barrel. You can un-jam your blaster or check to see if it is loaded by flipping open the jam-door, which is usually located on the top of the blaster above the trigger.

Safely Firing a Nerf Blaster

Safe handling of Nerf blasters can be excellent practice for children who will eventually learn to hunt with adult weapons when they are older. The principles of firearm safety should also be practiced with Nerf weapons.

1. Always treat the Nerf blaster as if it were loaded.
2. Don't point the blaster at somebody (who does not want to be shot).
3. Don't put your finger on the trigger, unless you are ready to shoot.
4. Only aim at the target zones of the other person (no head or groin shots)
5. Don't look down the barrel of the blaster (reminder)

These rules are very simple, so that even young children can understand them. The rules do not affect any of the fun of having an all-out Nerf war.

Honestly, most of the minor "owies" my kids have received during Nerf wars were due to getting overly excited and running into objects. We will talk about some ideas for preventing these types of injuries soon.

We have had some minor injuries with younger kids getting shot in the eye, which have resulted in short crying spells. But, even those kids quickly got over the minor pain with a short rub of the eye and they were right back in the battle.

Preventing eye injuries is the main priority of Nerf safety. Protective gear can prevent anybody from ever getting shot in the eye. But, the way that the user shoots the blasters can also ensure that nobody gets shot in the head.

First, never aim above the chest when you are shooting at another person. This can be very difficult when you are in a Nerf war and all you can see is the other person's head peeking up. But, you cannot take that shot!

Second, rules can be set that prevent head and groin shots. It's great when adults or older teenagers can be present to set rules and oversee battles. It is much easier than relying on kids to enforce the rules. We have tried making a rule that it anybody gets shot in the head that the war is over for the day.

Realistically, this does not work very well, because there are way too many situations that lead to kids getting accidentally shot inappropriately. Kids get excited. There are usually a group of kids running around and it is very common for them to get hit in the head.

Some more realistic ideas for reducing head shots and groin shots are to make rules that make it very bad to accidentally shoot another person there. You could make it a rule that you get taken hostage by the other team if you accidentally shoot somebody in an illegal body zone. You could also lose your favorite blaster for an illegal shot. Use your imagination and make it "painful" for the shooter to take a bad shot.

Another concern with some of the more powerful Nerf blasters is shooting another person at close range and/or when they are not expecting it. Even my wife whimpers when the Mega Centurion is aimed at her when the boys are too close. These types of blasters do sting when you get shot at close range and can leave light red marks on the skin.

Care should be taken to avoid shooting other people when they are too close to you. You should try not to shoot people unless you are at least ten feet from them and they know that you are shooting at them.

Protective Gear and Battlefield Safety

The easiest way to prevent injuries from accidentally getting shot in illegal areas is to wear protective clothing and other gear. Initially, children might think that wearing protective gear is "dorky", but that is not the case with Nerf blasters.

Wearing the correct type of protective gear can actually make participants in the Nerf war look more "real" – like actual soldiers, Star Wars characters, or G.I. Joe guys.

For younger kids, the protective gear can be a way for them to be creative. Let them develop their own gear that they wear for battle. You would be surprised what they come up with. My boys have made whole suits of armor from empty boxes and duct tape!

Here are some ideas for protective gear:

First, head protection or goggles to protect the eyes is the most important gear. You probably already have something at your house that you can use. For eye protection, we have used ski goggles, swimming goggles, swim masks, safety glasses and even an old paintball mask that we found at a Goodwill store for $1. For whole head protection, we have used old Halloween masks, Star Wars helmets, batting helmets with visors and catcher's helmets.

It can also be a good idea to cover bare skin when the bigger blasters are lurking. We like to wear long sleeve camouflage shirts and jackets and Star Wars costumes to keep from getting "stung". You may choose to wear light gloves, as getting shot in the fingers can also sting a bit.

Our kids also like to "pad themselves up" by putting additional padding inside their outer layer of clothing, but I think that it really is more to make them look like they have big muscles than it is to protect them.

Wearing shoes or other footwear is a good idea for indoor battles, as it is easy to stub your toe during battles and tennis shoes also prevent falls from slipping on smooth floors.

Battlefield safety is also important to consider before beginning the Nerf war. Again, it has been my experience that many accidents are results of how the battlefield is set up, not getting shot with a blaster.

Adults should check locations before battles begin to make sure that there are no sharp objects nearby. Rooms that have objects like power tools or glass objects should be off limits and doors should be closed (and perhaps locked).

For battles that take place outdoors, a perimeter should be set so that children do not get lost or find a patch of poison ivy.

When younger kids are part of the Nerf war, you should keep the lights on. Low-light conditions can be fun variations for Nerf wars, but having the lights off increases the probability of kids running into furniture or each other and also prevents accidental head shots.

One rule that can really help is the "Fast Walk Only" rule. Running is illegal under this rule and anybody that is caught running becomes a hostage or loses their blaster. Eliminating running during battles greatly reduces the chances of kids getting hurt.

After setting these rules for Nerf safety for one or two battles, kids get used to them being part of the process of having a battle and will automatically make them part of getting ready for future battles.

MODDING NERF BLASTERS

'**Mod**' is a slang word that Nerf blaster fans use to mean a **modification** (change) to stock Nerf blaster parts. Mods can be as simple as spray painting the outer surface of the blasters, or as complex as altering the interior firing mechanisms of the blasters.

Modding Nerf blasters has become a popular hobby for more experienced Nerf gunners. You can find hundreds of YouTube videos on the subject that cover many different custom mods. You can also buy modded blasters on eBay, usually at higher prices than the stock Nerf blasters.

Why would you want to mod your Nerf blaster? Some Nerf blaster owners want their blasters to look different than their friends' blasters, if they own the same models. Some people just like to tinker and see if they can make their blasters shoot faster or farther. Others are looking to add certain accessories that are not made for their particular blaster.

In *Nerf War*, we will talk about some reasons why you might not want to mod your Nerf blaster. If, after this discussion, you decide to alter your own blaster, at least you can say that you have been warned.

The bottom line is this: Young gunners should not modify their blasters without the help of a parent or an experienced modder.

My son Jackson watched dozens of videos on YouTube before deciding to mod one of his favorite blasters. It looked easy in the video.

Well, he got the blaster taken apart and removed a couple of springs, in an attempt to improve the reloading mechanism of his blaster. When he got the blaster put back together, it did not work like it was supposed to. He took the blaster apart and reassembled it several times and then finally lost several springs and had to throw the blaster in the trash. Lesson learned.

Most of the modders that put together YouTube videos are high school-aged teenagers or adults who have been making alterations to Nerf blasters for years. They make it look easy. But often, it is much more difficult to figure out exactly what is going on with very small interior parts than what it looks like in a video. You may not want to mod any blasters that work well. If you want to tinker, try modding a blaster that does not work well or you don't want anymore.

Reasons that you may not want to mod your Nerf blasters:

1. Mods can ruin your blaster.
2. It's easy to lose small springs and parts, after you take them off.
3. Many mods cannot be returned back to stock condition. If you cut the barrel on your Buzz-Bee Double Shot to make it a sawed-off shotgun, obviously you can't go back to having a full length barrel again.

4. Resale value. If you are an expert, modded blasters can make you some extra money when you sell them. HOWEVER, if the mod does not turn out perfect, you will not be able to sell your blaster. There are also many more customers looking to buy a stock Nerf blaster than a modded unit, so it will usually be easier to sell the stock models.

5. Safety. Blasters with modded actions can shoot significantly faster than stock Nerf blasters and CAN hurt people. They can also break fragile items. It is important to note that many modded blasters look much more similar to real blasters. Great care should be taken to ensure that they cannot be mistaken for real adult firearms (see below).

If you are looking to make an easy modification to a Nerf blaster, you can add many imaginative mods to the exterior of Nerf blasters, without affecting their shooting ability. My boys have added homemade slings, silencers and scopes that were crafted out of duct tape and cardboard. They looked really cool and were easily removed to return the blasters to stock condition.

They have also spray painted several blasters and those also turned out good. Just remember that once the blasters are spray painted, they are not considered stock for resale, even if you paint them back to the original colors. Also, if you paint the blasters, make sure that the muzzle is painted orange, so it is not mistaken for a real blaster from a distance.

FINDING NERF BLASTERS FOR CHEAP

One of the great things about foam dart blasters is that they are relatively inexpensive to buy new at department stores. Just yesterday, I saw a new Mega Magnus on sale for $12 at Meijer. You can buy a blaster that shoots well over 50' for just over $10!

Still, it can be a fun hobby trying to locate collectible blasters at bargain prices. For those of us with large foam dart blaster collections, it can also be fun attempting to locate blasters that we have not been able to shoot yet.

There are several places where you can routinely find used foam dart blasters for under $3:

1. Thrift stores – we have probably located 10-12 Nerf blasters at Goodwill and Salvation Army stores for $1-3 over the last year. These locations are also good places to find Nerf accessories like bipods, as the employees don't usually know what they are for and they will be priced 50c or $1. Just make sure that you test the blasters to see if they will fire. We take a small bag with a variety of darts and some batteries to test blasters, because there will be a significant percentage of blasters that do not work correctly at these places. Just load the blaster with a dart and shoot it safely into your parents' hand to test the firing mechanism.
2. Yard sales – Blasters found at yard sales will usually be very cheap. The problem with treasure hunting for blasters at these locations is that unless the yard sale host advertises that they will have Nerf blasters in their sales ad, you have no idea which sales will have

treasure. You could spend a lot of time and your parents could do a lot of driving to find what you are looking for.

3. Craigslist and local Facebook Sales Groups – Sometimes you can find good deals on Nerf blasters on these platforms. Craigslist and Facebook both have search functions, so you can search for 'Nerf' or 'darts' and find blasters at good prices. There are also Nerf Swap groups on Facebook, but you will usually not get a bargain price in those groups.

EBay and Amazon can also be good places to find rare or vintage blasters. Usually, you are going to be paying store prices, by the time you add shipping fees to the list price.

Amazon.com is the place to go, if you are looking for a particular blaster that is unavailable in stores. 80-90% of the blasters made in the last ten years will be available to buy on Amazon, but the rare blasters will not be cheap.

Selling your extra blasters can also be a way that you can buy new blasters for cheap. You can offset the price of a new blaster by making some money by selling blasters that you don't even use anymore.

It's very easy to sell used blasters on eBay. Just make sure that you describe the condition of the blasters accurately. Don't make the blasters sound better than they are, or the person that buys the blaster from you may leave negative feedback on the sale and then it will be much harder for you to sell items on eBay after that.

You can sell several different blasters together in a "lot", or a collection of blasters and accessories, in order to clear out a large volume of blasters and make some quick money.

It can also be very profitable to sell blaster parts to people that modify blasters. Several months ago, we found a Nerf Vulcan at a Salvation Army for $2 (Sweet!). We brought it home and messed around with it for a while, but could not get the firing chain to move. We won an eBay auction for a new Vulcan chain and a tripod for a couple of bucks. We tried the new chain in the Vulcan, but it would still only shoot one dart at a time.

Finally, we gave up. However, we made a very nice profit on the "dead soldier". We took apart the blaster and sold the parts on eBay. We sold the springs and screws for $8, the electric motor for $7, the tripods for $15 (on Amazon) and the good chain for $12 (on Amazon). We also still have the battery compartment and the handle that we have not listed yet, but will probably make another $10 on. That's $67 earned on a blaster that we only paid $2 for. Rock on! For further information on parting out free stuff for great profits on eBay, check out my book called Almost Free Money on Kindle.

FUN VARIATIONS FOR NEW FOAM DART BATTLES

Nerf wars are always fun, but as you become "veterans" of many foam dart battles, you start to want to try new variations to keep the experience fresh.

There are many fun and exciting variations that can add to your Nerf war experience. The variations can be weapons requirements, rules changes, or battlefields adjustments.

Here are several battles that can start your own creative processes, so that you can come up with your own unique foam dart battle variations.

Legal Blaster Requirements

Limiting which types of blasters are legal to use can really change how battles are fought. We have done a number of different battles with blaster requirement rules, such as: Pistols-only, Buzz Bee-only, Zombie Strike-only and Mega dart-only. With these rules, all other blasters are illegal to use.

Low-Light Battles

Dim lighting can really add to the atmosphere of the battle. It brings many new elements into the fight. It is much easier to hide from your opponents, so new hiding locations and bases can be used. It is much harder to hit your target, especially when the other teams' players are moving. These conditions also allow you to use some cool accessories, like laser sights and blinker bombs. These light-up accessories are much more useful in low-light conditions (plus, they look much more impressive).

As we discussed before, these low-light battles should only be done by older kids and with supervision. Young kids can get hurt by running into furniture or each other. A "fast-walk only" rule is usually effective in reducing the chances of injuries in these battles.

Care should also be taken to ensure that is not too *dark*. There has to be enough light to move around safely and see potential hazards.

The "Hunger Games" War

For those of you not familiar with *The Hunger Games*, here is the idea behind the popular book and movie, as modified for a Nerf war:

There are a number of participants who are fighting one-on-one to take each other out. Throughout the battle, weapons are found that can be used in the battle. The participants start out with only one basic blaster and can only use what they find over the course of the battle.

This battle variation works best outside in a large space. A person not involved in the battle hides a selection of blasters, bombs and/or accessories around the battlefield.

Participants in the battle start at opposite ends of the battlefield, out of sight of each other and the person that hid the goods.

When an audible signal is sounded, the battle begins. Participants must find their opponents and take each other out, using either their base blaster or the upgrades that are hidden on the battlefield.

An interesting variation to this battle is to have a "weapons depot" in the center of the battlefield that is overseen by a person not in the battle. Every couple of minutes, a new weapon is placed inside the depot and participants have to sneak in and get the new blaster or bomb before their friends get them. This weapons depot was a very important aspect of *The Hunger Games* story, as well.

This variation brings several new wrinkles into a Nerf war – one-on-one action, finding hidden treasure and tactical thinking (are participants going to go on offense, or hide and ambush moving opponents?).

Laser Tag-Style Battlefield

For those familiar with indoor laser tag businesses, you know that these places often have a bunch of barricades that players can hide behind. The barricades make Nerf wars really fun – you have to figure out how you are going to sneak into range, so that you are close enough to hit your enemies.

This idea can be applied to make fun outdoor battlefields, even in small yards. You can make a number of barricades out of two stakes and large flattened-out boxes or plywood at a very low cost.

Capture the Flag

Most kids are familiar with the game called Capture the Flag. In this battle, each team is given a flag that they must protect. If the other team gets their opponents' flag and gets it back to their base, they win.

If participants are hit with a dart in a core area (chest, torso), they are taken prisoner by the other team and put in "jail". They can only be released by being touched by a teammate. If they get hit in the leg or arm, that leg or arm cannot be used for the rest of the battle.

Again, this type of battle really encourages a lot of thought by participants. How are they going to get the other team away from their flag, so it can be captured? Is it a better plan to sit back and snipe, or go on the offensive? Should they use a "decoy" to draw out the opponents? This variation can be a ball!

"Fill 'em Fulla Foam!"

This is a very straightforward "battle". In this variation, you pick an unsuspecting adult target with a good sense of humor. You get as many friends and/or relatives as possible to help you. All of you fill up your blasters to full capacity (this works best with high-capacity automatic blasters, like the Hailfire and RapidStrike).

Everybody sneaks up on the target at the same time. When everybody is close enough, the leader yells "FILL EM FULLA FOAM!"

Then, everybody unloads their clips at the same time at the target, bombarding them with foam darts. The target's reaction is usually hilarious, especially if they are distracted, like when they are talking on the telephone or playing video games.

This is a lot of fun at birthday parties or family get-togethers.

Caution: This variation does not observe Nerf safety rules, as described earlier in this book. However, most adults are not going to be hurt or angry about being toasted. It's all in good fun. Just make sure that you are not shooting from less than 10 feet away. Also, the target should not be an elderly person or a pregnant woman. Care should be taken to avoid shooting anybody holding anything that could stain fabrics like the carpet, clothes, or furniture.

OUR FAVORITE NERF WAR STORIES

Nerf wars have provided us with many hours of family fun. Here are some of the highlights of our battles:

The Accidental Mom Head-Shot (Nolan)

Mom was wrestling with Jack, trying to capture him and take him to jail. Jack was on my team, so I was trying to rescue him.

In my mind, I thought, "Oh no, you don't!"

I cocked my Hammershot blaster and tried to shoot Mom in the hand, to break Jack out, but I accidentally shot her right in the forehead, between her eyes. We won the war.

Mom was laughing after I shot her in the head. It was funny.

'The Miracle Shot' (Eric)

I was upstairs in our house, set up to ambush the invading forces. Jackson engaged in a stealth attack on our team, sneaking up the stairs and unleashing a barrage of darts around the corner at our position. Then, he ran for the hills.

I pursued the attacker, chasing him back [safely] down the stairs. Jackson made it down the first flight of stairs and was heading for our lower level TV room and the protection of furniture barricades.

When I got down the stairs, I saw Jackson scrambling over top of a loveseat. If he made it over the loveseat, he would have been safe, as there is no way to shoot into the protected space behind it.

So, I had to take an impossible shot on the move, while still coming down the last couple of stairs. I leveled the Mega Magnus as Jack was clearing the top of the loveseat and I let the shot go from about 40-50' away. The Mega whistler dart actually sailed in an upward arc and then curved several feet to the right, hitting Jack just as he disappeared over the loveseat, taking him out with an incredibly lucky shot.

The dart had to be slightly misshapen from being shot so many times in order to curve like it did. A new dart never would have hit him, because the dart had to bend just right in order to get the angle necessary to get around the bannister rail in front of the chair.

Jack laughed, as he said "I can't believe that shot hit me!"

"I can," I said. "I'm that good."

The Recon CS-6 Mod Battle (Jack)

Before this battle, I had modded my CS-6 by making a homemade cardboard silencer and a scope and mounting them to the blaster. It took me about 40 minutes to make the accessories and attach them. They looked really cool mounted on the blaster.

The silencer that I made actually made the blaster's shot sound quieter and did not affect the range. The scope did not make the blaster shoot more accurate, but it made me feel more like a sniper in battle.

I carried the modded CS-6 into a night-time Nerf battle against Nolan. I saw Nolan coming up the stairs, because I had a green light sight attached to my scope which glowed to let me see Nolan in the dark.

I shot Nolan in the leg with the CS-6 and he went down. Then, I finished him off with a final shot to end the battle. This was one of my favorite battles because of the time I spent preparing my blaster for war and then the mods actually worked to take out my brother.

Improvised Incendiaries (Eric)

One of my favorite things about Nerf wars is the creativity involved in making battle plans. I like coming up with new and funny ways to take out the enemies. Some of the tactics involve making new kinds of fake explosives, or *incendiary devices*.

We use a bouncy ball with an interior blinker as a "bomb". The blinker is activated with contact, so I taped it to our dog's collar and tapped it with my hand, activating the "bomb". Then, I told Nolan to call Zeke (the dog) upstairs.

When Nolan called Zeke, he went upstairs with the activated "dog bomb" blinking, went straight to Nolan and took out both of the enemy soldiers, as Jack and I yelled "BOOM!" from our downstairs location.

Another time, I tried using a fake "plastique explosive" to take out approaching soldiers who were coming down the stairs to attack us. I taped together several of those "popper" New Year's Eve celebration noise makers. You know… the ones where you pull the string and they make a load 'pop' and shoot out confetti?

I taped the popper plastique "bomb" underneath the railing of the stairs and then ran a long string from the popper cords down the stairs and behind a protected wall, where I held onto the string.

When Nolan and Suzie came down the stairs, I yanked the cord to set off the confetti bomb and… nothing! A dud! The string came loose from the popper cords when I pulled it. The idea didn't work, but it was still funny to talk about after the battle.

The Useless Sniper (Suzie)

Eric and I were on a team against Jack and Nolan. We got all geared up and ready for the battle. We were downstairs and the boys were upstairs.

I made a sniper hide-out behind the couch, so that I could ambush the boys when they came downstairs. I waited there, aiming down the scope of my Mega Magnus with a blanket over me, waiting for action. I patiently waited and waited, like a real sniper while Eric battled both boys right above me in the kitchen.

Then Eric came down beside me, shooting it out with both boys on the stairs. I kept on waiting for a good shot with my Magnus. Finally, after over half an hour, Eric and the boys had shot almost all of their ammo in, like, all of their blasters. I took one shot and hit Nolan and then Jack took me out.

Eric and the boys shot off hundreds of rounds, using about ten blasters, while I hid under the blanket. I only got off one shot the whole battle.

NERF AND BUZZ BEE FIELD TESTS AND USER REVIEWS

Before we get into the field data that we put together for the field tests, we should discuss several things.

First, this information was gathered while shooting our own actual blasters. We used new darts when field testing, but some of the blasters had been shot for a period of time before the field tests. You may very well field test your own blasters of the same model and get slightly different results. New blasters that are fresh from the box will also have brand new springs and therefore shoot a bit farther than blasters that have been shot many times. You could also get different results based on the location the tests are administered, wind speed and direction, altitude, dart condition and the height of the tester.

For this book, we picked a variety of the most popular products to field test and review. There are dozens of Nerf and Buzz-Bee blasters out there and many of the discontinued blasters are hard to find and expensive. So, we focused on the blasters that most readers will be likely to find where they live without spending a fortune. We are planning to follow up this book with a sequel that would contain additional field tests of new and discontinued models.

We provide this information to help fellow Nerf gunners make informed decisions when they are getting ready to buy or sell blasters. Opinions provided are only that. Opinions. You should make your own purchasing decisions based on what you like and the type of blaster that you are looking to buy.

In order to field test for distance, we shot the blasters by holding them level with a 10-year old's shoulder (not elevated, in order to shoot the blaster into the air). The distance was measured on flat ground, based on where the dart hit.

For accuracy, we shot three darts at a 3-ring target 3'in diameter (a big target) with a 2" diameter tube for a center. We noted where the blasters hit the target when aimed very carefully and standing still inside, where there was no wind. We measured the distance from the center tube to where the dart hit the target. We used two distances for snipers – 20 feet and 10 feet. For most pistols, we used only the 10-foot distance.

For fear factor, we took into account the speed the blaster shot the dart, the projectile they fired and the overall appearance of the blaster (big tricked-out blasters are just more scary!).

All right! Let's shoot some darts!

Buzz Bee Blaster Field Tests

Model: <u>**Buzz Bee Air Warriors Extreme Range Master**</u>

Specs: 36" long, when assembled. Weighs 2.6 Lbs.

Has detachable scope, barrel and bipod. Package comes with 10 Buzz Bee suction cup sticky darts. The Extreme is advertised as being able to shoot up to 60 feet. The Extreme works with a pumping system, where the blaster can be cocked up to 10X to add speed and distance to the shots.

Field Test Distance: 30.93 Feet

Accuracy: 5.5" from center tube at 20'

Fear Factor: 8.8 (Eric 8.5, Nolan 10, Jack 8)

The Extreme's pumping action adds a nice Fear Factor effect to the blaster. Buzz Bee recommends a 10 pump maximum, but it makes other soldiers nervous when the blaster could be pumped up to 15 to inflict a stinging hit. The blaster has good range and accuracy and the size of the blaster is also impressive.

General Comments: The Extreme is one of Buzz Bee's most versatile blasters, as it can be assembled in several different ways, so that you can use it as a stationary sniper rifle or a mobile blaster in a war. When set up with the long barrel and the bipod attached, it looks cool set up behind a barrier as a sniper roost.

If you take off the barrel, the Extreme is actually quite light and shoots a bit farther. The range of just under 31' is conservative, as we have owned the blaster for over a year. The pump action of the Extreme seems to lead to a loss of distance over a relatively short period of time.

I highly recommend this blaster for battles because of the ability to use it as a stationary sniper and its modification aspects. Although Jackson does not like that you have to cock the blaster up to 10 times for maximum effect, I think that the cocking action with the bolt is fun because it is not used in very many other foam dart blasters. It makes the Extreme a nice change-up to the traditional Nerf blaster arsenal.

Jackson's Review: I think the Extreme is cool because it has good shot distance. But, I do not like that you have to cock the blaster more than once to shoot it a long distance. It also loses compression quickly after it is pumped up. I don't think that the Extreme looks as much like a sniper rifle as the Predator. It is not one of my favorite blasters.

Nolan's Review: The Extreme is one of my favorite blasters because it looks realistic and I like the action of the bolt. It looks like a sniper rifle when it is set up with the bipod. One thing that I do not like about the blaster is that the scope is really hard to get off of the blaster. The blaster is also hard for me to carry it when the barrel is on because it is too long.

Model: **Buzz Bee Double Shot Blaster**

Specs: 30" Long. 1.2 LBs

The Double Shot is a popular discontinued Buzz Bee model because the action works just like a real shotgun, with the cocking action and use of shells. The Double Shot can be found in an "over and under" vertical barrel alignment and also can be found in a "side by side" horizontal barrel arrangement. The side by side is collectible and often more expensive when found online.

In order to cock the blaster, darts are placed inside shells and then inserted into the barrels. The blaster is cocked by opening the blaster at the barrel (as seen in the photo) and then closing it. When the blaster is opened again, the shells eject, like a real shotgun.

You can shoot both barrels at the same time by giving the trigger a full pull, or you can shoot the dart from only one barrel at a time by pulling the trigger halfway.

The Double Shot features a secret compartment in the stock that can hold darts or other small items.

Distance: 18.5 Feet for double barrel shots.

The range can vary greatly with the Double Shot, depending on whether both barrels are shot, or just one barrel. It will shoot further with a single barrel shot. The range is OK for a multiple shot blaster.

Accuracy: 3.5" from center tube at 10'

Fear Factor: 3.5 (Jack 3, Nolan 3, Eric 5)

The boys say that the Double Shot does not inspire any fear from being hit with the darts themselves. It does not shoot fast enough to sting at all, even at close range. However, Eric felt that the double barrel capability and shotgun action added up to a moderate Fear Factor rating.

General Comments: The Double Shot is another of Buzz Bee's innovative blaster setups. We like the firing and cocking mechanisms and the fact that it resembles a real shotgun. It's really neat how the blaster ejects the shells after you shoot it. The hidden compartment is also handy for hiding additional darts, battle plans and other goodies.

On the downside, the action lends itself to breaking easily. There is a cord system that is used for cocking the blaster and it breaks easily. There are multiple reviews on Amazon about the blaster breaking and we had a Double Shot that snapped the shooting cord, as well. Overall, the Double Shot is a cool blaster, but the price has gone up to over $40 on Amazon due to its value to collectors. It has a surprisingly high 4.5 Star User rating.

Jackson's Review: I like how it looks like a real shotgun and uses shells, instead of regular darts. I did not like the Buzz Bee colors on the blaster, so I modded mine by spray painting it black and gray, which made it look much better.

Nolan's Review: I agree with what Jack said. I like how you have to open the blaster to cock it. But, I do not use it very much in battles.

Model: **Buzz Bee Predator Bolt Action Rifle**

Specs: 30" Long, 1.4 LBs

The main benefit of the Predator is how much it resembles a real-life bolt action rifle. The blaster is shaped exactly like a hunting rifle and the bolt action cocks like the real deal. It comes with 4 suction darts in the package. The Predator comes with detachable scope, which has limited aiming ability. It has a hidden compartment in the stock's end that holds 3 darts.

Distance: 18.9'

The Predator is advertised as being able to shoot "up to 30 feet" and it may come close to that distance fresh out of the box. For our field tests it was very consistent, firing 3 shots between 18 and 19.2'. Our Predator has been shot a lot over 2 years, so your new Predator may very well consistently shoot in the 25-30' range.

Accuracy: 3" from center tube at 10'

Fear Factor: 3.5 (Nolan 3.4, Jack 4, Eric 3)

The Predator looks sharp, which raised the Fear Factor a bit. But, there is no fear of being hit with the darts and the blaster only has a single shot action, so you only have to avoid one shot.

General Comments: The Predator has been a very consistent blaster over many battles. It always shoots straight and the distance is also consistent. You do not get many duds or sailing darts, like you do with many other Buzz Bee and Nerf models. Plus, it's easy to carry and can be used in pretend hunting play, as well.

The Predator is a sturdy blaster and one of Buzz Bee's most popular models. It has a 3.5 Star User Rating on Amazon and is #51 in Toy Dart Blasters in sales on Amazon.

Jackson's Review: The Predator is cool because it looks like a real sniper rifle. The single cocking action is better than the multiple cocking blasters like the Extreme Range Master. Aiming through the scope helps with shooting accurately.

Nolan's Review: I think that the Predator is a perfect size and weight for kids my size (7-8 years old). I like how you only have to cock it once for battles. I also like how the blaster looks like a real hunting rifle and the scope also looks realistic. It does have a long and hard trigger pull, though.

Model: **Buzz Bee Air Warriors Rogue**

Specs: 9.9" long, 10.4 Oz.

The Rogue is designed to be a one-hand pistol, but for smaller kids, it really ends up being shot with 2-hands. The size of the blaster is not ideal. It's too big to be used as a pistol in many situations and it is too small to be held like a rifle. However, it is lightweight and sturdy. We have found multiple Rogues at second-hand locations and they always shoot great.

The Rogue has a shooting action which is also awkward to be able to use it effectively as a pistol. 4 Darts fit on the end of the barrel and the dart assembly must be rotated each time the blaster is shot to get the next dart ready to fire (which again, means you have to use 2 hands to shoot this blaster in a war). The blaster is cocked with a slide on the top of the blaster.

The Rogue comes with 4 suction cup darts in the box. It has a 3 Star Amazon User Rating. This blaster is best used as a secondary weapon, although it has a powerful shot, as we will discuss shortly.

Distance: 27.5 Feet

Accuracy: 4" from center tube at 10'

Fear Factor: 4 (Eric 5, Jack 3, Nolan 4)

The Rogue may not look scary, but it can produce a bit of a sting when you get hit with the non-padded suction dart tips and it can "reach out and touch you" from well over 20' away. It also has a nice little 'pop' and kicks when it shoots, which adds to the Fear Factor when you are being targeted with the Rogue.

General Comments: Of the more than 25 foam dart blasters that we field tested, the Rogue probably surprised me the most. It shot well over 25', which is outstanding distance for a pistol (especially an older Buzz Bee model). The blaster that we field tested was a thrift store find and it still shot one used dart almost 29'! Brand new out of the box, this blaster can surely shoot well over 35'.

As mentioned before, the shape and action of the Rogue limits it usefulness in battle, but it is an impressive performer, in regard to its distance and velocity. Another advantage to this blaster is the price. You can find this blaster periodically at thrift stores for $1-2 and it is also very affordable on eBay and Amazon at under $10, including shipping.

This blaster is one of my favorite secondary weapons. It's a great blaster to have back at the base, for when your main blasters run out of ammo. The Rogue is easy to grab on the run because of its shape, easy-to-see color scheme and light weight frame.

Jackson's Review: The Rogue is not one of my favorite blasters, but I like the sound it makes when it is fired. I like the range, for a small blaster. I do not like the shape of the blaster or the twisting action of the barrel of the blaster.

Nolan's Review: I do not like how the Rogue looks, or the action. The blaster is also hard to cock.

Model: **Buzz Bee Rapid Fire Tek**

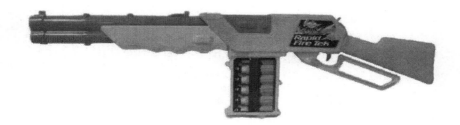

Specs: 29.6", 2 LBs

The Rapid Fire was marketed as a "Western Rifle" by Buzz Bee. It resembles an "Old West" lever action rifle, like those used by cowboys and buffalo hunters in the western US in the 1800s. The blaster is a cool-looking blaster, with a clip-fed lever action system that automatically ejects empty shells, which is awesome.

Out of the box, the Tek comes with 6 shells and darts and one clip. This blaster is getting really hard to find new. It costs over $115 on Amazon for a new blaster and even used blasters are over $35. The Tek is a collector's item. Grab it, if you see one for sale.

Distance: 10.5 Feet

Accuracy: Not tested, due to condition of our blaster.

Fear Factor: 2.5 (Eric 3, Jack 1, Nolan 4)

General Comments: The Tek is a really cool blaster to have in your foam dart collection. While it is a poor performer as far as the shooting distance, it does shoot accurately. The best part about this blaster is the action of the blaster. It is very unique, with ejecting shells and a lever action cocking mechanism, which is extremely similar to adult rifles. It also has a multiple-shot clip, which is an advantage in a war.

The Tek is an exciting find, if you can find one at a yard sale or thrift store, especially if you can find one with a clip (which we did several months ago).

The Tek that we field tested probably had a tired firing spring, so don't be too disappointed with the 10' range. Most models will probably shoot in the 15-20' range, which is still under-performing, in my opinion.

Jackson's Review: The Rapid Fire works like a real lever-action rifle and I like that the blaster has a clip and shells. The blaster shoots very straight and accurate. The lever has sharp ridges that hurt your hand a little when you cock it. I don't use the blaster in battles because of the short range and the blaster is hard to cock.

Nolan's Review: It looks a lot like a rifle and I like how it takes shells. I don't like the color of the blaster. I don't use ours in a war because it shoots bad, but it is a cool blaster to keep because it looks real.

Nerf Sniper Rifle Long Blaster Field Tests

Model: **Nerf N-Strike Mega Centurion**

Specs: 40.5" Long, 3.8 LBs

The Centurion is the largest Nerf blaster. It is hard for small children to carry it, but it is worth the effort in terms of firepower. When assembled, the Centurion is well over three feet long.

The blaster fires whistler Mega darts, which are loaded into a clip. The cocking mechanism is a sliding bolt action, which runs along the barrel in front of the trigger.

The Centurion comes with a bipod, a 6-dart Mega clip and 6 Whistler Mega darts. It comes in two color schemes – the red and white blaster shown in the photo and also a rarer "Sonic Ice" model, which is blue.

It is #23 on Amazon for foam dart blasters and has a user rating of 3.5 stars. It is priced at around $30-35 for a new blaster on Amazon, which is a good deal for such a powerful weapon.

Distance: 81.16 Feet

The Nerf ads claim that the Centurion will shoot over 100', which has been argued by many Nerf fans. Fresh out of the box, the Centurion will shoot close to that mark, but few owners have measured shots over 100 feet. Even so, the Centurion is the most powerful Nerf blaster that I have fired and the blaster is by far the most *effective* blaster at long range. It will regularly shoot 80 to 85 feet and it will shoot STRAIGHT and on target, which is a huge benefit in Nerf wars.

Accuracy: 3.5" from center tube at 10', 10.1" from center tube at 20'.

Fear Factor: 10 (Nolan 10, Eric 10, Jack 10)

The Centurion is the standard when it comes to Fear Factor. When we were deciding on Fear Factor values for the other blasters, we asked, "Well, how does it compare to the Centurion?"

The Centurion shoots faster and farther than any blaster that we have, plus it shoots Mega Whistler darts, which can put a real sting on you from up to 80' away and the whistlers sound scary when they are coming at you. The blaster itself also makes an unnerving sound when it fires, which adds to the Fear Factor.

You actually have to be careful when shooting at people at close range, because the "Mega" can leave a small red mark on bare skin, when you get hit. The Centurion is an impressive-looking Nerf weapon, due to its huge size. Even adults are scared of it.

Once you have been hit a couple of times with the Centurion at close range, you RUN when you see it coming in battle.

General Comments: The Centurion is awesome because of its shooting capabilities and intimidating appearance. While it is big and bulky to carry in battle, it packs a punch from a long ways out. It can also be set up as a base defense weapon by using it as a stationary blaster set up with its bipod and scope.

Many Centurion owners have had issues with it jamming up and darts getting stuck in the barrel when firing it. We have not had many jamming issues. If you rack the action all the way to the front while cocking it, you will have far fewer jams. I think that the majority of jams with this blaster are caused by short-armed users not giving the cocking mechanism a "full pull", and short-stroking the cocker. It does have a jam door for easy access to dart jams.

Jackson's Review: It's really big to carry. The cocker has a long pull to load it. It is probably good for kids over 10 years old. It works really well as a sniper rifle, if you put a scope on it (not included in the box). It shoots super far.

Nolan's Review: The Centurion is not made for little kids. It stings bad when you get hit with it. The cocker is really hard for smaller kids with short arms. The Centurion shoots really well.

Model: <u>**Nerf N-Strike Elite Rapidstrike CS-18**</u>

Specs: 24.5" Long, 3.5 LBs

The Rapidstrike boasts an automatic battery powered (Takes 4 'C' batteries) firing system, which shoots multiple darts when the trigger is held down. It will fire darts fairly quickly, using the interior motor, or you can fire individual darts with a single trigger pull. It comes with a large clear 18-Dart clip.

The stock is adjustable to make the blaster longer or shorter. The blaster does not come with a scope, but it does have a slide rail on top to be able to mount a scope later. It comes with 18 Elite darts in the box. The Rapidstrike has a 4-star user rating on Amazon.

Distance: 41.6 Feet

Nerf claims that this blaster will shoot 70 feet, but we have not experienced that distance, even when it was brand new. It has been a consistent shooter at 40-50 feet. Fresh out of the box, you may get shots of up to 50-60 feet. Even when this blaster was brand new, we did not see shots of nearly 70 feet long.

Accuracy: 0.3" from center at 10', 4.3" from center at 20'.

This blaster is a "pea-shooter". It is extremely accurate from both close range and at medium range distances. Jack field-tested it with a scope and hit the 2" wide center tube twice at 10' and once at 20'.

Fear Factor: 6.2 (Eric 7, Nolan 5, Jack 7)

General Comments: The Rapidstrike is an excellent all-purpose blaster for wars. The automatic firing system is really cool and it allows larger users to carry two blasters, as you do not have to cock the Rapidstrike after shooting it, until you run the clip dry.

It has an above average range and shoots very accurately, but its strength is being able to lay down a spray of darts for either cover-fire or offensive surges during battles. A Rapidstrike with several extra clips is an outstanding blaster to have on your side during Nerf wars.

Jackson's Review: The Rapidstrike is a good primary blaster because of the rapid fire [system] and lots of ammo in each clip. It can't be used as a sneak-attack blaster because the blaster makes a lot of noise (caused by the automatic firing mechanism). I like how the Rapidstrike looks like a machine gun.

Nolan's Review: It's cool because you don't have to cock it. It shoots really accurately. I think it looks like a real AK-47. I don't use it a lot in wars because it is so noisy.

Model: **Nerf N-Strike Elite Hail-Fire**

Specs: 23" Long x 12" Wide, 2.1 LBs

The Hail-Fire is one of Nerf's most unique blasters, featuring an innovative automatic battery-powered Accelerator firing system, with a rotating clip carriage on the bottom of the blaster. The clips are rotated by cocking the lever handle on the top of the blaster. The carriage holds up to 8 Quick-Load clips, so you can fit a heck of lot of ammo into it (up to 144 Elite darts, or even more with larger clips). It is advertised as being the "highest capacity Nerf blaster ever".

The Hail-Fire is fairly large and heavy, especially when loaded up with all 8 clips. But, you can shoot it for a long time without having to go back to base to reload ammo.

The Hail-Fire is fairly expensive, as is the case with most automatic firing system blasters. It is currently priced in the $50 range for new blasters in the box. You will also probably choose to buy extra clips and darts, as it only comes with four 6-round clips (you can use longer clips, like 12 or 18-round clips in it) and 24 Elite darts.

It has a 4-star user rating on Amazon.

Distance: 47 Feet

While distance is not the primary function of the Hail-Fire, it does have an impressive range of just under 50 feet. Plus, you can shoot multiple darts that distance in a very short time, with the Accelerator trigger firing system.

Accuracy: 1.67″ from center tube at 10′, 9.83″ from center tube at 20′

I was surprised at how accurately this blaster shot at close range. The blaster shoots very straight out of the muzzle, but it is difficult to aim due to its shape and the handle on top of the blaster. Still, Jack was able to hit the center tube from 10′ and hit the larger target each time from 20′, which would score body hits all three times at that range.

Fear Factor: 8.7 (Eric 9, Nolan 8, Jack 9)

The Hail-Fire's high Fear Factor rating is due mostly to its ability to fire a lot of rounds off quickly and accurately. When you see the Hail-Fire coming your way, you better take cover, or you will be taken out of the war.

The blaster shoots standard Elite darts, so you don't get the stinging effect of a Mega dart system like the Centurion, but you are much more likely to be eliminated from battle by the Hail-Fire from inside of 40′.

General Comments: The Hail-Fire is my go-to weapon in battles, especially if there are lots of people playing. When fully loaded, you can go on the offense for a long time and take out multiple targets. It is also great for base defense. You can put someone at your base with a Hail-Fire and who the heck is going to try to get in there?!

The cocking system for rotating the clips can be a little difficult when you are running or trying to change out clips quickly, but you can also rotate the clips manually with your hand. It does get hard to tell if the clip you are rotating into firing position is full or empty after you rotate the clips a couple of times.

The firing system itself is awesome. It shoots darts fast, hard and straight. I remember very few instances of dart jams and this blaster gets used a ton. There is not really an aiming device, but it is used more to "spray" darts toward your opponents, anyway.

Jack and Nolan do not like the Hail-Fire's automatic firing system as much as the RapidStrike's, but I prefer the Hail-Fire, as you can actually shoot rounds off faster by pulling the trigger yourself than you can with the RapidStrike's system that shoots by holding the trigger down.

This is probably my favorite Nerf blaster and it has taken out a lot of enemies.

Jackson's Review: The Hail-Fire is a good primary blaster because you can hold a lot of ammo. The firing is not as good as the RapidStrike because you have to pull the trigger every time you shoot (instead of holding the trigger down).

I like my blasters to look more like real blasters, so the Hail-Fire is not one of my favorites. I also like to snipe more and the Hail-Fire is more for running around and shooting. The trigger is also a little bit hard to pull.

Nolan's Review: It's a really cool blaster because it holds 8 clips. The blaster is not really automatic because you have to pull the trigger every time. I like the handle on top for holding the blaster and switching the clip. I like the Hail-Fire, but Dad uses it a lot in wars.

Model: **Nerf N-Strike Elite Recon CS-6**

Specs: 17.1" long, 2.7 Lbs.

The Recon comes with a detachable stock and barrel, which makes it a very popular model, due to its adaptability. It also comes with a flip-up sight, which fits on a slide rail on the top and a red-dot laser sight for night battles. The Recon can be used as a rifle or disassembled and used as a pistol. It shoots Elite darts and uses the standard clips, which are interchangeable with other Elite blasters.

The Recon is cocked with a slide on the top of the blaster. It has a top jam door, to make it easier to clear jams. It has a 3.7 User Rating on Amazon.

Distance: 36.7'

Our Recon had a fair amount of darts shot through it, before this test. The Recon has shot consistent distances for the several months that we have owned it. It has not lost distance. Fresh out of the box, you are probably looking at distances of 40-45'. We fired one dart at 41' during our field tests

Accuracy: 4.2" from center tube at 10', 11.3" from center at tube at 20'.

Fear Factor: 4.4 (Eric 5, Jackson 4, Nolan 4)

The Recon does not have much of a sting to it, but it is a solid performer in battle. Ours has taken out many soldiers.

General Comments: The Recon is the blaster that is picked first in many wars. It fits smaller frames perfectly with the stock on and it has the ability to be used in a lot of different ways. You can use it as a primary rifle, or as a secondary pistol. Plus, it just looks cool and it is easy to load and fire. The night sight is also functional for close range shooting in low-light conditions. The Recon is a staple of many Nerf arsenals.

Jackson's Review: The Recon is cool because it has a lot of attachments. You can change the looks of the blaster by adding different accessories. I like the yellow and gray colors. The blaster does not have the best range or accuracy. When all of the attachments are on, it looks like an AK47. The blaster jams way too much, so I do not use it a lot.

Nolan's Review: I like the looks of the blaster. It looks really cool when you put a scope on it. I like how it cocks on the top with the slide, but it jams very easily.

Model: <u>Nerf Zombie Strike SlingFire</u>

Specs: 26.5" Long, 2.2 Lbs.

The Slingfire is probably the most popular blaster in the Zombie Strike series, which features exterior design schemes related to popular culture zombie shows. The Slingfire comes with 6 green Zombie Strike darts, but it will also fire the standard sized Elite Darts (as will all Zombie Strike blasters).

The Slingfire comes with a 6-Dart clip. It is cocked with a lever-action located on the bottom of the blaster. The Nerf commercials and YouTube videos show the Slingfire being cocked by holding onto the lever and swinging the blaster forward with one hand. This can be done fairly easily by older owners, but it is difficult for kids under 12. I can cock the blaster in that manner, but it does not cock correctly every time when attempting the one-handed motion.

It also has a jam door on the top of the blaster. It has a 3.5 star User Rating on Amazon. You can find the blaster for around $20 new online. It also comes in a Limited Edition package, which includes a 25-dart drum.

Distance: 40.7'

The Slingfire shot very consistently, with all three shots measuring within 2 feet. This blaster shot farther than we thought it was going to shoot on the range.

Accuracy: 5.3" from center tube at 10', 13.2" from center tube at 20'

The problem with the Slingfire is that there really is no way to accurately aim the blaster. There is a barrel sight, but nothing to line it up with.

Fear Factor: 6.7 (Eric 5, Jackson 8, Nolan 7)

The fear factor is middle-of-the-road for the Slingfire. It shoots for a good distance, but it is not very accurate and does not have any sting, when you get hit with it. The unique cocking motion adds to the fear factor.

General Comments: The Zombie Strike blasters are really sharp looking blasters, in my opinion. Just for that fact, I like having the Slingfire in the arsenal. The lever action cocking system is also a fun variation to shoot once in a while. As far as usability, this blaster is not going to be a primary blaster in battles very often, as it is a single shot weapon (with a 6-dart clip) which takes longer to reload than most blasters.

The blaster's size and design make it easy to carry for smaller kids and it is fairly light.

Jackson's Review: The Slingfire is one of my favorite blasters. The lever action is fun to use and it's the only Zombie Strike that has a clip system. You should buy the blaster, if you do not have it. The stock's design makes it easy to aim. The Slingfire looks really cool with a scope on it. I really like the blaster, but it jams up quite a bit.

Nolan's Review: It's the only stock blaster that I have seen that lets you open the jam door when it is still cocked. I also like the lever action. It shoots pretty good. I like the design of the blaster and the looks of it. It looks like it has a wooden stock.

Model: <u>**Nerf Zombie Strike SledgeFire**</u> Shotgun Blaster

Specs: 25.2" Long, 1.6 LBs

The Sledgefire has a design that is very popular with Nerf users. The Zombie Strike exterior and 3-dart shotgun firing system makes it a Nerf favorite.

The blaster comes with 3 shells, which can each be loaded with 3 Zombie Strike or standard Elite darts. The shells can be stored on the shell holder system on the stock of the blaster. The blaster is loaded by opening the barrel of the blaster and inserting one shell (each shell contains 3 darts). Upon pulling the trigger, 3 darts are fired at once, shotgun-style.

The Sledge has a very high 4.7 star user rating on Amazon. The blaster can be found new online in the $25-30 range.

Distance: 38.17'

The Sledgefire that we used had about 2 months of usage before testing. It has been a consistent shooter in the 38-40' distance, which is surprising, considering the firing style of the blaster. This blaster will reach out and touch you from over 40' away on occasion, although at that distance, you will get a fairly wide spread of the three darts, making it difficult to consistently hit targets.

Accuracy: 5.3" from center tube at 10'

We only shot this blaster at 10' because the three dart firing system makes the darts spread out too far beyond that distance. Even at 10', you get a wide variance in how the blaster shoots the darts. It's a shotgun and its purpose is to cover a larger area. Accuracy is not very important for this style of blaster.

Fear Factor: 6.7 (Eric 6, Nolan 4, Jackson 10)

The Fear Factor is increased because of the 3-shot ability and the appearance of the blaster. It can also hit you from a long distance. Jack rated the Fear Factor a 10 when the blaster has new darts, because getting hit by 3 darts at close range can "put a hurtin' on ya".

General Comments: I like the overall design of the Sledgefire. It is a unique blaster that shoots 3 darts and the shell holder on the stock is helpful. I enjoy the process of shooting the blaster. It's a fun blaster to fool around with. The way that the blaster opens up and has to be loaded with the shell holders is unlike any other Nerf blaster.

Although the design is interesting, I personally do not like the color scheme of the Sledge. It also has limited usage in battle, due to the time it takes to reload the blaster. Once you shoot the 3 shells, the blaster is rendered useless, as it takes too long to place the darts inside the shells and then reload it into the blaster.

The Sledge can be used very well as a base defense weapon. It sprays 3 darts and can hit more than one target at a time.

The blaster does have good range, but accuracy outside of 15′ is unreliable. Most users buy this blaster more for the experience of shooting the blaster and its appearance than for using it in Nerf wars.

Jackson's Review: I like the shell idea. It's the only Nerf blaster that I have used that works that way. The shells make it more like a real shotgun. I wish that it cocked more like the Hammershot.

I really like how the Sledgefire feels in your hands when you are in battle with it. I feel like other players are afraid of it, so I feel good when it is in my hands. You can take out three people at the same time with it.

Nolan's Review: I like the Sledgefire because it seems to work like a real shotgun when you load it. I also like how the darts spread out when it is shot to hit a wider target. I like how the shells are stored on the stock. I like carrying it in battles because of the grip on the stock and the size of the blaster.

Model: **Nerf N-Strike Elite Roughcut 2x4**

Specs: 18.9" Long, 1.2 LBs

The Roughcut 2x4 is another great Nerf design. It shoots either 1 or 2 darts with each trigger pull. 8 darts are loaded into the barrel of the blaster. It can shoot 2 darts at a time and 8 darts total, without reloading. The blaster can also be fired one barrel at a time by pulling the trigger halfway, which allows the shooter to very accurately fire the blaster (see below).

The blaster is cocked with a pump-action slide on the bottom of the blaster, which makes the blaster function like a double barreled shotgun.

The blaster also features an N-Strike Elite tactical slide on the top of the blaster, so that owners can mount an Elite scope on it (although it does not come with one in the box).

The Roughcut 2x4 comes in three color schemes – white and orange (Whiteout), blue and white and Zombie strike design (which is available in a 2-blaster pack). It can be found for about $20 new online ($35 for Zombie Strike package) and has a solid 4.2 star user rating on Amazon.

Distance: 42.3'

The Roughcut is advertised as being able to fire over 75 feet, but even when this blaster was brand new; it never shot over 60' for us. It shoots consistently in the 40-50' range. Our longest shot on the range was 46' after owning the blaster (bought brand new and only shot less than 30 times) for about two months. We also had shots on the range of less than 35', even with brand new darts.

Realistically, this blaster is primarily a shotgun. The distance outside of 40' does not matter much, as the spread of the darts would make it difficult to hit a target at that distance if both darts are fired, anyway.

Accuracy: 0.5" from center tube at 10', 6.7" from center tube at 20'

When this blaster is fired one dart at a time, it is an extremely accurate performer at close and medium ranges. Jackson hit the center tube 2 out of 3 times from 10' and the third shot was only 1.5" from the tube. It was the 2nd most accurate blaster that we tested on the range, which surprised both of us.

Fear Factor: 6.7 (Eric 7, Jackson 6, Nolan 7)

This blaster is an outstanding shooter and inspires fear, when you see an opponent shooting it. The 2-shot function and ability to shoot off 8 shots very quickly also adds to the Fear Factor of the Roughtcut 2x4.

General Comments: The Roughcut 2x4 gets used a lot in our Nerf wars. It is easy to carry and is a sold multi-purpose weapon. It can be used as a shotgun, firing two shots at long distances, or it can fire one shot at a time very accurately at distances up to 50′.

Another benefit is that the blaster is easy to load by sliding up to 8 darts into the barrel holders. It's very convenient to be able to scoop up other gunners' fired darts and simply reload the 2x4 on the run during battle.

It's also very lightweight and easy to carry for all sizes of Nerf fans. It can be used one-handed by older users, allowing you to carry two blasters in battles.

The only drawback of this blaster is that the darts fall out of the barrel holders fairly easily if the blaster is tipped downward (this happens fairly often when running) or when it is jarred (like when you are getting into position to shoot). This can be overcome by holding your hand over the darts, but doing that makes the blaster a two-handed weapon.

Jackson's Review: I like the Whiteout series color scheme. The pump action is cool – it works like a pump action shotgun. I wish that the blaster did not load in the front, because the darts fall out when you are using it. The grip is nice and I like how it does not have a stock because it makes the pump action easier to use.

Nolan's Review: I like how the darts look in the front of the blaster. I don't like how the blaster does not have a stock. It makes it harder to aim and it's harder to keep the blaster steady. I like to be able to shoot at two people at the same time and the pump action is fun to use.

Nerf One-Handed Blaster Field Tests

Model: **Nerf Zombie Strike FlipFury Blaster**

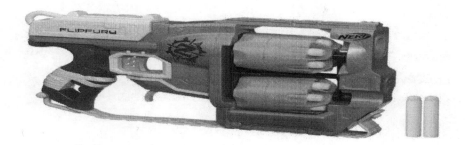

Specs: 15" Long, 1.9 LBs

The Flipfury is the first Nerf blaster with two barrels, which allows you to shoot 12 Elite or Zombie Strike darts without reloading. The blaster is loaded from the front of the barrels. The barrels rotate and fire darts when the upper trigger is pulled. The lower trigger is used to transfer from firing from one barrel to the other, without having to reload. The blaster is cocked with a slide on the top of the blaster.

The Flipfury is a very popular Nerf model. It is the #1 selling Nerf blaster, as I write this book. It has a very high 4.8 star user rating on Amazon.

Distance: 64.5'

Brand new out of the box, this blaster has excellent dart velocity and shot distance, although we had a wide variety of distances fired from one loading of the barrels. The majority of the darts landed in 60-64' range, but we also had two darts in the 58' range and one that sailed over 70'.

Accuracy: 0" from the center tube at 10' (3 hits), 3.4" from center tube at 20' (2 hits)

You would not think that this would be one of the most accurate Nerf blasters, if you just look at the design of the blaster. There is not a great sight line to aim the blaster with. However, it was the most accurate blaster that we tested. Jackson shot 2 darts inside the center tube from 10' away and hit the outer edge of the tube several more times.

Fear Factor: 8.4 (Eric 8, Jackson 8, Nolan 10)

The Flipfury inspires a high Fear Factor with the appearance of the blaster and also with its performance. You can shoot 12 rounds off quickly and the blaster shoots very accurately from both close range and also from longer distances away.

General Comments: The Flipfury is the #1 Nerf blaster for a reason. It shoots great and it looks cool, with its vertical double-barrel shooting system and Zombie Strike design. The blaster is the most accurate model that we tested and it shoots a long ways, especially for a one-handed blaster. The Flipfury is a great bargain at only $20 at most stores.

Jackson's Review: The Flipfury is cool because it is light and it holds a lot of ammo. The barrels flip very smoothly and quickly. You should buy the blaster because it is a great bargain, it shoots accurately and also shoots long distances.

Nolan's Review: I like the Flipfury because the two barrels make the blaster look awesome. I gave it 10 Fear Factor because it can shoot a long distance and shoots very fast out of the barrel. I don't really like the wrapping design on the handle, but I do like the rest of the orange and gray Zombie Strike design.

Model: **Nerf N-Strike Elite Mega Magnus**

Specs: 14.9", 1.9 LBs

The Mega Magnus is a powerful one-handed blaster. It shoots the larger Mega darts, so it packs a punch. The blaster is cocked with a slide on top of the blaster. It holds 3 darts in the integrated interior clip, which is loaded from the port on top of the blaster.

The Magnus has a 4.6 star user rating and is a big seller on Amazon. It is a bargain at under $10 in most stores and online locations.

Distance: 54.5

The Magnus is advertised as being able to shoot up to 85 feet. We measured consistent distances of between 52 and 56 feet, although our Magnus has been fired many times and still shoots great. Fresh out of the box, the Magnus will shoot well over 60 feet.

Accuracy: 0.6" from center tube at 10' (2 hits), 3" from center tube at 20' (1 hit)

Fear Factor: 8.7 (Eric 8, Jackson 9, Nolan 9)

The Magnus shoots Mega darts at an impressive velocity for a one-handed blaster, so it can put a sting on you. It also shoots very accurately, all the way out to over 40'.

General Comments: I think that the Mega Magnus is the best overall value for any Nerf blaster. You can find it new on sale for around $5, every once in a while. The blaster is incredibly accurate and is very easy to load. Because you simply feed darts into the top port, you can easily reload while in the middle of a battle, even in low-light conditions. The Magnus is light and it is a very comfortable size for smaller kids. It hardly ever jams. The only negative aspect of the blaster is that it only holds three darts and must be re-cocked after each shot.

Jackson's Review: I like the Mega Magnus because it holds multiple darts without needing to have a clip. The blaster also shoots very accurately in battle. I like it more than the Centurion because it shoots close to the same distance, but it is much cheaper. It's also very easy to reload.

Nolan's Review: I like the Mega Magnus because it holds three darts and does not need a clip. When you cock the blaster back, you can stick darts through the top tube and then fire them. One bad thing is that the way that you load the Magnus makes the darts get smashed easy.

Model: **<u>Nerf N-Strike Elite Strongarm Blaster</u>**

Specs: 13" Long, 1.1 LBs

The Strongarm features the "Slam Fire" function, which allows you to quickly fire all 6 Elite darts in the rotating clip by holding down the trigger and racking the slide back and forth. The blaster also features a tactical slide rail on top, so that you can attach Elite accessories, such as a scope (not included in box). The blaster comes in several colors, including white and blue (Whiteout) and a red Sonic Fire color scheme.

The Strongarm is a very popular blaster, because of the Slam Fire ability and low cost ($10-12 new). It has a strong 4.6 star user rating on Amazon and it is the #2 blaster in the Foam Dart category.

Distance: 46.9'

The Strongarm is advertised as being able to shoot 75'. Realistically, after a short time out of the box, you will get in the range of 45-50', if the blaster is held level and fired. It is a strong performer at that distance, especially for a one-handed blaster.

Accuracy: 3.4" from center tube at 10' (1 hit)

Fear Factor: 6 (Eric 7, Nolan 5, Jackson 6)

The Fear Factor is raised for this medium sized blaster, due to its ability to shoot very quickly with the Slam Fire function. It also has good velocity out of the barrel.

General Comments: The Strongarm is a staple of most Nerf gunners' arsenal. If you don't have one, you should buy it, since you can pick one up for about $10. The blaster shoots fast and straight and the Slam Fire is fun to mess around with. It also has the ability to add a scope, which makes the blaster much more appealing.

The Strongarm is light for a medium sized one-handed blaster. It is easy to load and cock, for gunners of any age.

Jackson's Review: I don't like the Strongarm as much as the Maverick because the Strongarm grip hurts your hand when you cock it. The Strongarm has a sweet sight that makes the blaster shoot really accurately. I like how the revolver clip can flip out partway to let you load it easier. If you are a revolver person, go get the Strongarm. If not, get something else.

Nolan's Review: I like the action on the Strongarm because it is easy for me to fire it. I like the blasters that cock on the top like this blaster and the Sidestrike. It works a lot like the Maverick, but it has Slam-fire.

Model: **<u>Nerf Zombie Strike Doublestrike Blaster</u>**

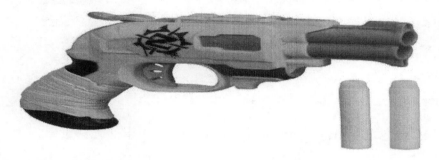

Specs: 9.2" Long, 7.8 Oz

The Doublestrike features the Zombie Strike design and easy to load and shoot functionality. The blaster is loaded by placing two Elite or Zombie Strike darts in the muzzle of the blaster. It is cocked with the thumb lever on the back of the blaster, which preps the blaster for taking two back-to-back shots without re-cocking or reloading.

The Doublestrike has a solid 4.3 star user rating and can be found for under $10.

Distance: 40'

The Doublestrike was very consistent, with 3 shots between 38 and 41'. It has very good distance for a pocket sized blaster.

Accuracy: 2.33" from center tube at 10'

Fear Factor: 6 (Eric 5, Nolan 9, Jack 4)

Nolan said that his Fear Factor rating was so high because it hurts when you get hit by the Double Strike at close range.

The Doublestrike is a sharp looking pistol and has very good velocity out of the barrel. It packs a punch, for a pocket sized blaster.

General Comments: I really like the Doublestrike, as a secondary blaster. You can easily stash it in your gear or large pockets and it is very easy to reload in battle.

It does have some limitations, with the two shot capacity and the muzzle-loading style that makes it more likely that the darts will fall out while in your pocket.

I like the general design of the blaster and how it looks like a real revolver, although the lime green color is not my favorite.

Jackson's Review: The Doublestrike is good for sneak attacks because of its size and it is easy to cock. It's a good blaster to hide on you, for when you get taken prisoner. It has a really good grip for younger users, like under 10 years old, especially.

Nolan's Review: I like the Doublestrike because it fits in your pocket good and I like how the darts fit in the front of the blaster. It shoots accurately and hits you hard.

Model: **Nerf N-Strike Triad EX-3 Micro Blaster**

Specs: 4" long, 5.6 Oz

The Triad is a pocket-sized pistol blaster that allows the user to load it with three Elite or Zombie Strike darts by placing darts into the three slots in the muzzle. The blaster is cocked using the pull handle on the bottom. When the trigger is pulled, the Triad shoots one dart. Then the user must re-cock the blaster to shoot again. The Triad will shoot from each of the three muzzle positions without needing to be reloaded. It has a very good 4.6 star user rating.

Distance: 51.7'

This blaster shot over 50' after owning it for over a year and using it almost every battle. It is advertised as being able to shoot up to 75'.

Accuracy: 3.8" from center tube at 10'

Fear Factor: 5.4 (Eric 6, Nolan 5, Jackson 5)

You wouldn't think such a small blaster would have a good Fear Factor rating, but the Triad's rating is fairly high because of its ability to be hidden so easily, plus it has 3 shots and can take out enemies up to 50' away.

General Comments: I carry the Triad in battle every time that it is available. It is a steal at $5-6 new. It shoots over 50 feet and it is a pocket blaster with three shots. You can hide it almost anywhere – your pocket, in your sock or boot, or in your backpack. This allows you to carry an extra blaster, in case you get captured or run out of ammo with your other blasters.

I love this blaster. It is very easy to reload and it shoots a long ways. It shoots basically the same as the Jolt, but you can load 3 darts, instead of only one (with the Jolt) and it costs about the same.

The only drawback is that the cocker takes some force to get it all the way back into firing position, although Nolan has been able to easily cock it since he was 6 years old.

Jackson's Review: It's a good blaster to use because of the three shot ability. It's great to have three shots, in case you have to shoot more than one person when you are breaking out of jail. It also has great range. It's very small, so it can fit in any sized pocket.

Nolan's Review: It's cool because it can hold three darts in firing position. I like the pull cocker because it cocks in one motion, instead of having to rack it forwards and then back.

Model: **<u>Nerf N-Strike Elite Firestrike Blaster</u>**

Specs: 5.2", 9.9 Oz.

The Firestrike shoots one Elite or Zombie Strike dart at a time. The blaster must be cocked using the pull handle on the back of the blaster. It has two muzzle slots for storing two additional darts, although the blaster will not shoot the darts from the storage slots.

The Firestrike features a laser sight, which is used to sight in on targets up to 15' away. The laser sight is turned on using the smaller trigger located underneath the primary shooting trigger. The Firestrike also has a tactical slide rail, so that you can add Elite accessories like a scope (not included in box). It has an excellent 4.6 Star rating.

Distance: 49.3'

The Firestrike shoots about the same as the Triad. We had one shot of over 56'. It will occasionally shoot over 60'.

Accuracy: 4.3" from center tube at 10'.

Jackson used the laser sight to aim with and it was not all that accurate, even from 10' away. It is an accurate shooter, if you do not use the laser sight.

Fear Factor: 5 (Eric 4, Jackson 4, Nolan 7)

General Comments: The Firestrike has excellent range, with the ability to shoot up to 50-60'. The laser sight is a cool feature and the ability to add a standard Elite scope is also handy.

That being said, the Firestrike is primarily a pocket pistol. When compared to the Triad, it is larger and harder to hide and it only shoots one dart at a time (without having to be reloaded from the storage slots). It also costs a bit more and shoots very similarly, as far as distance and accuracy.

I prefer the Triad, although the Firestrike's laser sight is cool in low-light battles and the ability to add accessories makes it more versatile than the Triad.

Jackson's Review: The laser sight is nice for when you are wandering around in dim light. I like the cocking mechanism. I also like the front grip for holding the blaster. The laser sight is not very accurate for aiming the blaster, though.

Nolan's Review: I like the extra dart storage, but I don't like how it only shoots one dart at a time without reloading. I like the double triggers. The trigger that turns on the laser sight is cool.

Model: <u>Nerf N-Strike Dart Tag Magstrike AS-10</u>

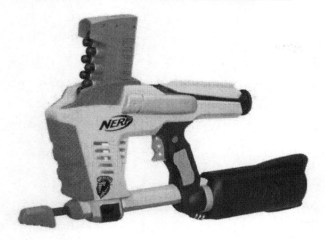

Specs: 22.5 Long x 10" Tall, 3LBs

The Magstrike is an impressive-looking blaster, capable of shooting 10 Dart tag darts "UZI-style" (rapid-fire sub-machine blaster). After loading 10 darts into the clip, the blaster is pressurized by pumping the handle on the bottom of the blaster up to ten times. Compressed air is held in the storage tank at the back of the blaster. The blaster will shoot the standard Elite darts, but performance can be affected.

When the trigger is held down, the stored air pressure fires all darts in the clip very quickly, shooting a spray of darts at your target. The Magstrike has a 4.0 star user rating.

Distance: 34.5'

Accuracy: 2.5" from center tube at 10'

Both Jackson and I were very surprised at how accurately this blaster shot at close range!

Fear Factor: 9 (Eric 9, Jackson 9, Nolan 9)

The Fear Factor of the Magstrike comes from the blaster's ability to take out multiple targets very quickly. It shoots 10 darts in less than one second when the tank is fully pressurized and it shoots very accurately at close range. The appearance of the blaster is also unique and a bit intimidating. If this blaster shot Mega darts, it would have received a 10 from Eric.

General Comments: The Magstrike is getting harder and harder to find. If you can find one, they are a riot to shoot, when they are working right. The blaster shoots off ten darts in a hurry! You can hold off a whole army of bad guys by laying down a line of "suppression fire" with the Magstrike.

It is worth noting that these blasters are prone to not firing correctly. The compression tank seals can go bad and the clips can also have problems. Sometimes, the whole clip will not fire at once. The Magstrike that we have starts losing compression fairly quickly (after a minute or so).

But, all in all, this is a great Nerf blaster. If you can find one, they are well worth the extra cost to buy. They are a ton of fun to shoot and very effective in Nerf battles for either offensive or defensive tactics.

Jackson's Review: The Magstrike is awesome because of how fast it can fire darts. Pumping the action takes a long time to get it ready to fire and I don't like how the compression releases pretty fast after you pump it up.

Nolan's Review: I don't like the look of the top loading clip.
I don't like the style of shooting because it is hard to tell
where you are shooting the darts.

Model: <u>**Nerf Zombie Strike Crossfire Bow Blaster**</u>

Specs: 16.5" Long x 12" Wide, 1.6 LBs

The Crossfire shoots exactly like a real crossbow. Pull the bow back with the handle cocker above the trigger and then it shoots one Elite or Zombie Strike dart at a time from the muzzle of the blaster.

The Crossfire holds up to 4 darts at a time, but only shoots once per trigger pull. The blaster is designed in the popular Zombie Strike color scheme. Fans of 'The Walking Dead' love this blaster, as a crossbow was used often in the TV show.

Distance: 32.7'

This blaster shoots significantly shorter than advertised right out of the box and it also tends to lose bow string tension fairly quickly with use. But really, this blaster is not bought for shooting distance, so who cares? It shoots far enough to play around with.

Accuracy: 5.6" from center tube at 10'

Fear Factor: 5 (Eric 4, Nolan 6, Jack 5)

Pretty weak-shooting blaster, but it does look a bit scary.

General Comments: The real draw (no pun intended) of this blaster is that it is a crossbow and it is fun to shoot. The Crossfire does not have any advantages to other blasters in a Nerf war. Really, it's bulky to carry and does not shoot as well as most other blasters. Like most other muzzle-loading blasters, the darts easily fall out of place during battle if you do not hold them in with your hand while moving.

The Crossfire is more of a "novelty" blaster. It's cool to look at and fun to shoot, but not useful in battle situations.

Jackson's Review: I think that it's cool because it was the first crossbow Nerf made. I like how it holds 4 darts. It stinks that the darts always fall out, which is why I do not use it very much in battles. But, it shoots accurately in fights.

Nolan's Review: I don't like how the darts fall out of the front of the blaster when you are cocking it. I like how the action is like a real crossbow. I don't use it much in battles because of the darts falling out all of the time.

Model: **<u>Nerf N-Strike Maverick Rev-6</u>**

Specs: 12.1" Long, 1.2 LBs

The Maverick comes with 6 suction darts in the box, but it will also shoot the standard Elite darts and Zombie Strike darts. The Maverick boasts a flip-down revolver-style rotating clip that holds up to 6 darts at a time.

The blaster is cocked with the slide on top of the blaster and then the blaster will fire once. It must be cocked again before each shot. It has a tactical slide rail on top, so that an Elite scope can be attached (not included in box). The blaster comes in two color schemes – yellow-and-black and white-and-blue.

The Maverick was designed to look like futuristic versions of Old West cowboy blasters and the appearance has been very popular with Nerf fans. The blaster has a solid 4.3 star user rating.

Distance: 28.7'

Our tired old Maverick has had many rounds fired through it. You can expect decent distances out of the box – between 35 and 45'.

Accuracy: 4.6" from center tube at 10'

Fear Factor: 5 (Eric 4, Nolan 5, Jackson 6)

The Mav doesn't have a high Fear Factor compared to some other blasters. It has below average distance and accuracy, but hey, it's a Maverick and you have to own one if you are a true Nerf fan.

General Comments: The Maverick is "the old stand-by" of Nerf blasters. Almost everybody has shot one. We have found 3 of them at thrift stores for under $2 and they always shoot perfectly. They are incredibly durable blasters and never jam. They are very easy to shoot and reload and they are a perfect size for smaller Nerf gunners.

The Mav is not an exceptional bargain at $15-20 new, compared to some of the newer blasters that shoot farther and more accurately, but everybody should own a Maverick at some point. Look for them used at yard sales and thrift stores for under $3.

Jackson's Review: My friend Mason has a Maverick and his shoots really well, because he got it new. It hurts when you get hit with it. I really love the Maverick because it is really easy to cock, it has 6 shots and every shot you take is a direct hit. It's one of my favorite overall blasters and a great secondary blaster.

Nolan's Review: When a Maverick is not new it stinks, because it loses distance quickly. It is cool because of the revolving clip. I think people should buy it because it is good size for 9 or 10 year old kids and older.

Model: **Nerf N-Strike Mega Bigshock**

Specs: 7.5" Long, 8.5 Oz

The Bigshock is the Mega version of the Jolt blaster, with more power and shooting distance. The blaster is a palm-sized pocket pistol that fires the larger Mega whistler darts. The blaster only shoots one dart, plus it can hold one additional dart in the extra storage holder on top.

If you are buying this blaster online, make sure that you are buying the US version of the Bigshock which has the orange trigger and not the less powerful gray-triggered blaster, which is made in Australia.

The Bigshock has a 4.3 star user rating, but the rating would probably be closer to 4.6, if a number of 1-star ratings from people that received the weaker gray-triggered model were removed.

Distance: 64'

Accuracy: 0.3" from center tube at 10' (2 hits)

Fear Factor: 8 (Eric 7, Nolan 9, Jackson 8)

The Bigshock puts a sting on you from a long way out. For such a small pistol, it really packs a punch.

General Comments: We just picked up the Bigshock, so I have not had a chance to shoot it much in battles. It seems to be an excellent little blaster. It is slightly larger than the much weaker Jolt, but it is still plenty small enough to conceal almost anywhere.

As far as pocket pistols go, the Bigshock packs a much larger blow because it shoots the Mega Whistler darts. It shoots farther than the Elite model pistols and only costs $1-2 more. It's a great blaster for under $10.

Jackson's Review: I like the Bigshock's size. It allows you to carry it anywhere in battle. The blaster is easy to cock and I like it much better than the Jolt because it shoots the Mega darts and shoots harder.

Nolan's Review: It works like the N-Strike Elite Jolt pistol, but it's better because it shoots farther and harder. The Bigshock's dart holder is cool because you can use it for a sight.

Model: **Nerf Zombie Strike Sidestrike Pistol with Holster**

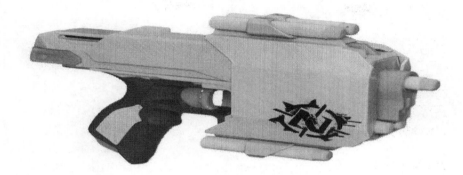

Specs: 12", 12 Oz

The Sidestrike is a one-dart pistol blaster, with the added advantage of having a holster that clips onto your belt or pants. The holster holds an additional 4 darts. The blaster itself holds three darts – one in the muzzle and two in storage slots below the muzzle.

The blaster cocks using a slide located above the trigger. After shooting the first dart, you have to take a dart from one of the holders and load it into the muzzle to fire it. The Sidestrike has a 4.6 star user rating.

Distance: 29.6'

Accuracy: 4.2" from center tube at 10'

Fear Factor: 4.3 (Eric 3, Nolan 7, Jackson 3)

General Comments: There are a number of better options for pistol blasters than the Sidestrike, in my opinion. Unless you are one of those "Zombie Strike guys", you will probably decide to buy a pistol that is easier to hide (like a Triad), or is a better shooter (like a Mega BigShock). The Sidestrike actually costs more online than the other pistols mentioned, as well.

The cool thing about the Sidestrike is drawing it from its quick-strike holster. It does feel awesome to pull the blaster out of the holster and shoot it. If you have friends who also own a Sidestrike, you can duel "Old West" style and see who can draw and shoot the fastest.

Jackson's Review: The Sidestrike is a good secondary blaster and it can be held with a holster. I like how it looks like a real gun.

Nolan's Review: The Sidestrike is cool because it is our only blaster with a holster. The extra dart holders are helpful, too.

Nerf Disc Shooter Field Tests

Model: **Nerf Vortex Praxis Blaster**

Specs: 18.6" (27" with the stock attached), 2.6 LBs

The Praxis has a 10-disc clip that is fired by cocking the blaster with the pump action below the muzzle. The clip is removed by holding down the thumb lever near the trigger. The Praxis has an Elite tactical slide rail on top, so that accessories can be added. The stock can also be removed so that the blaster is shorter and easier to carry. It comes with 10 foam discs.

The Praxis has a 4.4 star user rating.

Distance: 55.8'

Accuracy: 8.7" from center tube at 10', 11.3" from center tube at 20'

Fear Factor: 6.3 (Eric 4, Nolan 9, Jackson 6)

Nolan gave the Praxis a 9 because of the awesome design of the blaster, plus it shoots well.

General Comments: The Praxis is a sharp looking disc shooter, which has the advantage of being able to use it either with the stock for more accuracy or without the stock for ease of carry. It can also be used with a scope, although it does not come with one in the box.

I am not a huge fan of the disc shooting blasters, but I do like the Praxis. It has good range and disc velocity out of the barrel.

Jackson's Review: I like that the Praxis takes a clip. It's really easy to get the clip out. I like the pump action and how it works. I recommend the Praxis, if you can find it for under $30.

Nolan's Review: I like the pump action on the Praxis. I also like how the clip drops right out of the blaster when you press down on the thumb release. My Praxis has the Sonic Neon Green color, which is rare and cool. It does jam pretty easily when you Slam-fire it.

Model: **Nerf Vortex Pyragon Blaster**

Specs: 21" Long x 12" Wide, 4.3 LBs (without discs)

The Pyragon features a 40-disc drum clip, which makes it the highest capacity disc blaster, as this book is written. Surprisingly, the Pyragon comes with enough discs in the box to fully load the blaster (40).

The blaster is cocked using the pump at the front of the blaster. It can also be "Slam-Fired", by holding down the trigger and racking the pump.

The drum is removed by pushing down on the thumb lever near the trigger. You can also swap out the drum with a standard 10-disc clip, which makes it lighter and easier to carry.

The Pyragon has a tactical rail, so that it can accept Elite accessories (not included). It has a 4.6 star user rating on Amazon.

Distance: 50'

As is common with disc shooters, the Pyragon shoots fast and hard from close range, but discs sail when shot at targets that are further away. We had shots from 43′ all the way out to 56′, depending on how straight the discs flew after they left the blaster.

Accuracy: 6″ from center tube at 10′, 11.3″ from center tube at 20′

Fear Factor: 7.3 (Eric 7, Nolan 9, Jackson 6)

With its 40-disc capacity and Slam-fire capability, the Pyragon can shoot a lot of discs at your opponents very quickly. The discs don't sting at all, but they get on you in a hurry. You can take out a whole army of opponents in short order.

General Comments: The futuristic appearance and high capacity of the Pyragon make it a great disc blaster to own. If you only buy one disc shooter, the Pyragon is a good choice. The price of the disc shooters is usually higher than the dart blasters and that holds true with the Pyragon, which currently costs about $40 on Amazon.

The Pyragon is getting harder to find, so you may be the only one of your friends that owns one, if you decide to buy it online.

Jackson's Review: I like the drum clip on the Pyragon. It holds the most discs of any Nerf disc shooter that I have seen. I like how it has Slam-fire. I use it quite a bit, when I have enough discs to fill it up.

Nolan's Review: I like the Pyragon because it holds 40 discs and it has Slam-fire. The front handle feels really cool in your hand and it's easy to cock and shoot. I like it better than the Praxis because the Slam-fire on the Pyragon does not jam.

Model: **Nerf Zombie Strike Ripshot Disc Blaster**

Specs: 11" long, 12 Oz

The Ripshot is the entry-level Zombie Strike disc blaster. It comes with 3 foam discs. To shoot the blaster, one disc is loaded into the barrel and then the back slide is locked back to cock it. After firing the blaster, you must manually slide the action forward, load another disc into the barrel and then cock it back again.

There is additional disc storage in the front of the blaster, but you cannot fire discs from those slots. The design is the original green and orange Zombie Strike scheme, which appeals to some Zombie Strike collectors.

The Ripshot has a 3.9 star user rating.

Distance: 45'

Accuracy: 5.6" from center tube at 10', 12" from center tube at 20'

Fear Factor: 2.7 (Eric 2, Nolan 3, Jackson 2)

The Ripshot fires "sailers". The discs come out of the barrel slow and they sail, if there is any wind at all. The blaster is also slow to reload.

General Comments: The Ripshot is widely considered to be one of Nerf's worst firing designs. The action is very awkward and difficult to get cocked into the correct position to fire the discs. It's a single disc shooter and you have to load each individual disc into the muzzle before firing it. I do not recommend this blaster, unless you find it used (like we did), or you want to round out your Zombie Strike collection.

Jackson's Review: The way it cock and fires is weird. I like how it can hold three darts, but overall I do not like the blaster. It was way overpriced when it was new. It was almost $50 at the store when it was new. Don't buy the Ripshot. The cocking mechanism takes forever to cock.

Nolan's Review: I don't like the Ripshot because you have to cock it back and then stick a disc in and then shoot. The blaster's size is good for smaller kids, but it does not shoot very well.

Model: **Nerf Vortex Nitron Disc Blaster**

Specs: 25.5" long, 3.1 LBs without batteries

The Nitron was the top-of-the-line disc shooter when it was introduced and it is still one of Nerf's coolest overall blasters, which is why it is so hard to find.

The Nitron features an included pulse laser scope and a high-capacity 20 disc clip. The blaster fires discs rapidly, with its battery powered automatic disc firing system, which is fired by simply loading in the clip and holding down the trigger.

Distance: 45'

Accuracy: 8.7" from center tube at 10', 13.7" from center at 20'

Fear Factor: 6 (Eric 7, Jackson 6, Nolan 5)

The Nitron shoots a spray of discs quickly, taking out an opposing army in no time. It would have a higher fear factor, but the foam discs have no sting at all to them. The only "fear" is getting taken out of the war by getting hit. The Nitron is the most intimidating disc shooter, due to its size and automatic fire ability.

General Comments: The Nitron is my favorite disc shooting blaster. The automatic firing system is really fun to shoot. You can spray a fan of 20 foam discs by holding down the trigger. The laser scope is also an excellent addition and it is an advantage in dimly lit battle locations, like basements.

The Nitron is one of the larger and heavier of Nerf blasters, especially after you get the 6 'C' batteries, 2 'AAA' batteries and discs loaded into it.

At close range, the Nitron is devastating. Fast-moving foam discs are very hard to avoid, especially when there are 20 of them in the air at once!

Jackson's Review: The Nitron is cool because of the machine gun action. I recommend the blaster for all kids 9 and up, because it is too big for kids under 9 to carry. The battery pack is way too heavy, too. Its shoots pretty far but is not really accurate.

Nolan's Review: The Nitron is way too big and heavy for small kids like me, but it shoots really good at close range.

FIELD TEST DISCUSSION

The process of shooting a bunch of foam dart and disc shooters and measuring their performances was very interesting. It was a lot of fun shooting blasters with the boys and talking about Nerf and Buzz-Bee blasters with them.

There were a lot of blasters that shot significantly farther than we thought that they would shoot. Some blasters came up short.

One thing is for sure. We did our best to provide you with accurate information, so that you can decide on which blasters are right for you. Would we have liked to have been able to field test all of the newest and best blasters? Sure.

Unfortunately, we could not afford to buy a bunch of brand new blasters, so we tested what we had available to us. Luckily, we had a lot of popular blasters to shoot!

Several things are important to remember about the field tests:

1. We shot the blasters like YOU would shoot them. We did not shoot them to make them fit what Nerf ads or YouTube videos claim these blasters will do. We shot the blasters held level and measured where they hit the ground. We did not fire the blasters into the air to see how far they would shoot, because that would not help you to judge how they would perform for you.

2. The field tests provide <u>realistic</u> information that you can use to make decisions. We shot our own blasters that had already fired some rounds through them before the field tests. You get a great idea about how the blasters will perform over the entire life of the blaster. Tests on blasters fresh from the box are interesting, but they don't tell the whole story. How do these blasters hold up over time? What do people who have shot the blasters many times really think about them? <u>That</u> is the real benefit of these field tests.

3. There are some human elements in these field tests. The blasters were fired by a 10-year old young man – a gunner that is representative of the average Nerf fan. These tests were not performed in a laboratory, or by an overzealous adult. I'm sure that the testing process did not yield *scientific* data. The blasters were probably not fired at exactly the same angle. Jackson is an outstanding Nerf marksman, but he probably aimed some Nerf models better than others. The point is… these tests are guidelines only. They are for fun, not for arguing about.

Thanks for reading our book! We enjoyed talking about foam dart blasters with you and hope that you got some valuable information from it.

APPENDIX 1: TOP 10 BLASTERS BY DISTANCE

BLASTER	DISTANCE
1. Nerf N-Strike Mega Centurion	81.16'
2. Nerf Zombie Strike FlipFury Blaster	64.5'
3. Nerf N-Strike Mega Bigshock	64'
4. Nerf Vortex Praxis Blaster	55.8'
5. Nerf N-Strike Elite Mega Magnus	54.5'
6. Nerf N-Strike Triad EX-3 Micro Blaster	51.7'
7. Nerf Vortex Pyragon Blaster	50'
8. Nerf N-Strike Elite Firestrike Blaster	49.3'
9. Nerf N-Strike Elite Hail-Fire	47'
10. Nerf N-Strike Elite Strongarm Blaster	46.9'

APPENDIX 2: TOP 10 BLASTERS BY ACCURACY AT 10'

BLASTER	DISTANCE FROM CENTER
1. Nerf Zombie Strike FlipFury Blaster	0" (3 Hits)
2. Nerf N-Strike Elite Roughcut 2x4	0.2" (2 Hits)
3. Nerf N-Strike Mega Bigshock	0.3" (2 Hits)
4. Nerf N-Strike Elite Rapidstrike CS-18	0.3" (2 Hits)
5. Nerf N-Strike Elite Mega Magnus	0.6" (2 Hits)
6. Nerf N-Strike Elite Hail-Fire	1.67" (2 Hits)
7. Nerf Zombie Strike Doublestrike Blaster	2.33" (1 Hit)
8. Nerf N-Strike Dart Tag Magstrike AS-10	2.5"
9. Nerf N-Strike Elite Strongarm Blaster	3.4"
10. Nerf N-Strike Mega Centurion	3.5"

APPENDIX 3: TOP 10 BLASTERS BY FEAR FACTOR

BLASTER	FEAR FACTOR
1. Nerf N-Strike Mega Centurion	10
2. Nerf N-Strike Dart Tag Magstrike AS-10	9
3. Buzz Bee Air Warriors Extreme Range Master	8.8
4. Nerf N-Strike Elite Hail-Fire	8.7
5. Nerf N-Strike Elite Mega Magnus	8.7
6. Nerf Zombie Strike FlipFury Blaster	8.4
7. Nerf N-Strike Mega Bigshock	8
8. Nerf Vortex Pyragon Disc Blaster	7.3
9. Nerf N-Strike Elite Roughcut 2x4	6.7
10. Nerf Zombie Strike SlingFire	6.7

APPENDIX 4: TOP 10 BLASTERS BY AMAZON STAR RATING

BLASTER	STAR RATING (OUT OF 5)
1. Nerf Zombie Strike FlipFury Blaster	4.8
2. Nerf Zombie Strike SledgeFire	4.7
3. Nerf N-Strike Elite Mega Magnus	4.6
4. Nerf N-Strike Elite Strongarm Blaster	4.6
5. Nerf N-Strike Triad EX-3 Micro Blaster	4.6
6. Nerf N-Strike Elite Firestrike Blaster	4.6
7. Nerf Zombie Strike Sidestrike Pistol with Holster	4.6
8. Nerf Vortex Pyragon Blaster	4.6
9. Nerf Vortex Praxis Blaster	4.4
10. Nerf N-Strike Mega Bigshock	4.3

THANK YOU, READERS!

Thank you for taking the time to read this book. I hope that you enjoyed it as much as we enjoyed writing it.

Click on the link below to sign up for our newsletter and receive 3 free full-length Eric Michael bestsellers. You will also be notified about upcoming book releases in this series!

http://forms.aweber.com/form/75/228725575.htm

If you have any questions, please contact me at the Almost Free Money Facebook page, or on Twitter. I would enjoy hearing from you!

If you feel that this book has helped you and your family, I humbly ask you for only two things. #1, tell your family and friends about this book, and #2, please take several seconds to leave positive feedback for this book on its Amazon Detail Page.

Positive feedback directly affects other readers' reviews and leads to additional orders, and the proceeds from this book will go directly into my sons' college funds. Thanks again, and happy blasting!

ADDITIONAL LINKS

Eric Michael Author Central Page

EricMichaelBooks.com – Over 80 pages of free internet selling tips and thrift store flipping ideas

Book Titles in the Almost Free Money series:
Etsy Empire: Proven Tactics for Your Etsy Business Success, Including Etsy SEO, Etsy Shop Building, Social Media for Etsy and Etsy Pricing Tips

#1 Amazon Bestseller in E-Commerce and Crafting categories.

Passive Income for Life: A Time-Tested Secret Recipe for Building a $50,000 Cash Machine on Amazon.com...In Your Spare Time

Almost Free Money, volume 1: How to Make Significant Money on Free Items That You Can Find Anywhere, Including Garage Sales, Scrap Metal, and Discarded Items

#1 Amazon Kindle Bestseller: Almost Free Money has appendices that contain over 540 items that can be sold and specifies where to sell them for maximum profit with numeric and textual eBay categories.

Copyright, Legal Notice and Disclaimer:

Made in the USA
Lexington, KY
10 September 2015